Mastering Account Management

102 Steps for Increasing Sales, Serving Your Customers Better, and Working Less.

By Dan Englander
www.SalesSchema.com

ISBN-13: 978-1500958930
ISBN-10: 150095893X

Table of Contents

Introduction

The *account manager* title is rather amorphous. This fact makes the role compelling: you can make the job what you will. You can learn and apply skills that fall outside your day-to-day. That's how you develop a powerful edge.

Maybe you're in advertising, and your world is all about exceeding customer expectations and winning big pitches. Perhaps your realm is software, and your goal is not only acquiring new users, but understanding your customer's journey and working with your development team to improve your product. Your product might be of the physical nature, and you're focused on landing new accounts and strengthening your relationships with existing customers. Or, like mine, your product might be project-based, and you're focused on acquisition, project management, and farming new business. Your specific title might be Customer Success Manager, Account Executive, or something different. You might be a hunter, farmer, or something in between.

Regardless, this book will make you better at what you do. Through succinct steps, it will give you the know-how to acquire more business, serve your customers better, and work more effectively.

Sales will be a big part of this book, and you can benefit greatly from a sales-oriented mindset even if you're not a salesperson, per se. Understanding sales will allow you to comprehend your customer's needs. If your goal is getting feedback or product validation, winning a pitch, getting more favorable terms from a manufacturer, or simply making sure a project goes smoothly, a sales mindset will help you along. Though many of the examples in this book are based on hunting new business, the lessons can be applied to all sorts of undertakings.

For consistency, I use "products" to represent both products and services. If you're in a service business, then you might consider your "product" to be your time. Regarding "customers" and "clients", the former usually refers to transactional sales, and the latter to professional services or relationship-based business. The lessons in this book are applicable to both groups, granted the purchase is large enough to require a sales process. Since a client is a customer, but not necessarily the other way around, I will use the term "customers".

My Story

I started my journey into account management in the New York advertising world, handling digital marketing for customers like Marc Ecko, Monster Cable, and Big Ten Network. I was on the client services side of a boutique ad agency, and there was an iron wall between me and the sales people who brought in the business. Though I learned how to manage projects and keep clients happy, I didn't know how to find potential for new business. When I did identify opportunities, I was unprepared to sell. I didn't like it when clients were dropped on my desk without any explanation as to how or why they were there. I wanted to generate new business and keep it churning, and I wanted motivation from fat commissions. Suffice to say, I began looking for a new job.

I found an online ad for an account manager position at a new animation studio in Midtown Manhattan. The studio was a one-man shop, founded and led by its creative director. The founder carved out a successful niche, creating high quality explainer videos for tech startups. The new account manager would be the first employee in a company that would grow to many more. His or her duties would be one-third sales, one-third marketing, and one-third project management. I was intrigued.

After a successful interview process, I landed the gig. From the get-go, I enjoyed learning about our prospects' products and making recommendations over the course of speedy sales calls. The cognitive challenge of conceptualizing complex offerings enlivened me.

Although I had little sales experience at the time, I plodded along and met our goals. I was able to bring in a passable number of customers. My "sales process" went something like this: Prospects called or emailed us for pricing details. I then gathered the basic information and sent them quotes. We won some deals like this, but I wasted a lot of time compiling materials for people I'd never hear from again. After setting more ambitious sales goals, I realized I didn't have the skills needed to rise to the next level.

After some instruction and constructive criticism, I stopped wasting time on quotes and proposals for those who would never buy. I learned how to prospect and send emails that convert. I began to farm business with existing customers. After applying these new skills, I grew our revenue to nearly $1 million in year two, tripling our first year's target. In addition to a who's who of tech startups, I began to add large organizations like Showtime, Bank of America, Verizon, and Electronic Arts to our customer roster ... not too shabby for a two-person animation shop.

Though we had some big wins, I realized that as I put all my efforts into bringing in business, my service to existing customers suffered. Fires sparked up and expectations were flubbed. In the process of prioritizing sales, I had the subconscious naive notion that if the product was stellar at the end of the day, the path to it, however bumpy, didn't matter.

Thankfully, I had plenty of opportunities for trial and error so I could figure out how to land new business while keeping existing customers happy. This book will teach you what I've learned. It will give you the tools you need to become a successful account manager because it's centered on specific approaches and techniques, including email templates, phone scripts, and spreadsheet structures. While these materials are specific, they can be repurposed to fit your industry.

Resources

Throughout the book, I reference tools and additional materials found on our **Resources** page (www.SalesSchema.com/Resources). For convenience, please take a second to **bookmark this page**. Also, please **join the newsletter**, found in the right hand column, to stay up to date on new tools, apps, and strategies.

Managing Time (Steps 1-5)

Regardless of your industry, account management is about doing a lot of different things well. Let's say you read the rest of this book and you take the lessons to heart. In the course of winning at one thing, you might drop the ball somewhere else. For example, maybe you start to serve your existing customers better, but then you turn around and your sales pipeline is shrinking. Maybe in the course of acquiring new customers, you neglected to develop metrics on retention and activation. Or perhaps serving your largest key account made you forget about the smaller fish, and they start looking elsewhere for the next new model. In this section, we'll focus on ways you can avoid such predicaments by managing your time and keeping your stress level down.

Step 1. Create 2-3 Missions

Your missions represent your overall goals. Depending on your industry and position, the number and nature of your missions may vary, but generally you should have 2-3. For example, you might focus on closing new business and serving existing customers (like the account manager in the next example). Or maybe your missions are split between creative strategy and meeting client needs. Regardless, they should be important broad goals that encompass a variety of tasks.

Try breaking all your priorities into 2-3 overarching missions for your industry and position. These missions will guide the flexible tasks you do every day, which we'll get into next.

Step 2. Develop a Flexible Schedule

Flexibility is powerful. Success comes from motivation, and the best way to kick start motivation is through small victories. The best way to achieve small victories is by focusing on the task that excites you at any given time.

Below is a prototypical schedule for an effective account manager. The white bullet points are flexible, but the black points, representing the overarching mission, stay consistent each day. Though this example is for a project-based account manager who is both a hunter and a farmer, you can repurpose it for your position.

- 9 a. m. – 12 p.m.: **Generate new business**
    - o She looks over emails from the previous evening and only opens messages from prospects. She spends 30 minutes - 1 hour fielding these leads.
    - o She uses the Inbox Pause app to halt the flow of incoming mail.
    - o She spends one hour doing research and another sending emails to targeted prospects.

- 12 – 1 p.m.: **Meet customer needs**
    - o She answers customer emails, delegates tasks, and makes sure projects are moving along without hiccups.
    - o After answering all customer emails, she writes or updates the status line for each project in Asana, a web app for keeping track of project management tasks.

- 1 – 2 p.m.: **Lunch!**

- 2 – 3 p.m.: **Generate new business**
    - o She assigns a small research project to her virtual assistant in the Philippines (more on this later).

- 3 – 4 p.m.: **Open period**
    - o She schedules unavoidable calls during this block.
    - o If no meetings or calls, this time is spent planning or performing a marketing task. Today, she finds a conversation in Quora (www.quora.com) related to her product and offers helpful advice, linking to her company's site.

- 4 – 4:30 p.m.: **Meet customer needs**

- o She deals with any pressing customer issues that can't be deferred until the next day's email binge.

- 4:30 – 5 p.m.: **Generate new business**
  - o She writes and sends follow-up emails and proposals to well-qualified prospects.

Step 3. Batch Your Tasks

The human brain isn't built to jump erratically between unrelated tasks. Transition time is required. This is especially true in respect to account managers, who are constantly multi-tasking. When you focus on one goal at a time, you will generate serious momentum.

With that in mind, try to get things done in quick succession; don't spread out the annoyances of petty or tedious tasks. If you have to respond to customer emails, wait for them to pile up over the course of 4-8 hours. Go down your list of messages and fire off your responses. If you have to complete an admin task, like filing vendor invoices, do it all in one sitting.

Step 4. Limit Email

Email is an addiction. Dopamine is shot into your brain with the anticipation of each message (source: Psychology Today). This is why all parties involved in the culture of email encourage urgency. In reality, as you might discover after neglecting your inbox for a few days, very few messages are truly urgent. When an immediate response is needed, you can be reached over the phone.

But as an account manager, email is your lifeblood. It's the hub of your sales and customer service processes. So how do you turn it off? Well, you don't entirely. Rather, you control it. Here is an effective method for limiting your email intake:

Read and send emails no more than 3 times a day (as covered above).

Set expectations about when you will be checking email with your superiors, colleagues, and customers. Don't ask for permission; just say, "I've been very distracted by email lately, so I will be checking it at 9:30 a. m., 12 p.m., and 4 p.m. I know I'll be more effective with this schedule, and I'm confident I can meet everyone's needs." Include a note about your email-checking schedule in your signature line.

Be disciplined with the email checking periods you establish. Although you will experience withdrawal at first, stay strong to wean yourself off of the addiction.

Use email apps to limit inbound messages, like Inbox Pause (more in **Resources**).

Step 5. Limit the Phone

To cut back on this distraction, screen customer calls during sales time, and the same with sales calls during customer service periods. Get comfortable with politely deferring incoming calls. Like email, the implied sense of urgency with phone calls is often misleading. If you have to defer a prospect to later in the day, chances are you won't lose the business. We all learn to deal with other people's schedules, and most will understand when you're unable speak at a requested time.

Serving Your Customers (Steps 6-21)

Customers love you when you demonstrate that you understand their needs, and they don't want to perform an aggravating amount of legwork getting you to that level of consciousness. This section will show you how to find out what your customers are expecting, which isn't always intuitive.

The things that go wrong during a customer engagement may seem unique at first glance, but usually they have happened before and will happen again. With that in mind, we'll cover a process for identifying, anticipating and putting out fires.

There are some customers that will be all too content with breaking your usual process. Be firm with these people.

Step 6. Value Customer Experience, Not Final Output

When I first started at my company, I had the vague notion that the quality of the finished product was all that mattered. At the end of the day, I thought that as long as the work is great, the rest can go out the window. Many account managers share this opinion, perhaps subconsciously. Boy, was I wrong.

I had a particular project go south because I was unable to give a customer the experience they were expecting. This customer, who was creating several commercials for an automotive company, wanted numerous thumbnails, storyboards, and finished art before allowing us to create the animatic (a rough animated cut). His demands were beyond what we were willing or able to deliver. In hindsight, we probably would have forgone the business if we had understood what he wanted. In the end, the final deliverables were superb by all accounts, but there was little chance we would work together again. Our time would have been better spent fostering a long-term relationship with someone else.

Step 7. Know When to Be Proactive and Reactive

At a previous job, I was told to be incessantly proactive with my customers. I was to tell them the status of everything at all times. They were supposed to have every possibility laid out in front of them. Though we were building Facebook apps and running media campaigns (I think cake-baking is a delicious metaphor), I would say, "Right now we're selecting the flour for the cake, and then we will choose the yeast, and the icing, including its color and composition, and then the fruit topping, and then the oven, and then the serving plate …" In hindsight, I know I was doing all parties a disservice.

Irrelevant details distract your customers and plant the seeds for over examination and stress. To offer a great customer experience, be proactive about the areas you know cause concern. Be reactive about the less common concerns when they pop up.

Step 8. Understand Expectations

Managing expectations is about fulfilling your customer's vision and patching up differences before they cause problems. I used to think that customers would tell me what they were expecting. I was mistaken…. Articulating our conscious and subconscious needs is often beyond our ability as humans. Whether we are purchasing a sandwich or a website, we have expectations that exist below the surface. As an account manager, it's important to understand expectations so you can manage them, and this comes from prying them out by asking questions.

You will be in a great position to understand expectations if you're involved in the qualifying phase of the sales process, which we'll get to later. If the sales process is outside your purview, you should still interview your customer to learn as much as you can about what they are expecting from the engagement. With that in mind, start by asking questions like the following, ideally in person or over voice. The below questions and others in the following steps should guide your interview.

As I'll mention more than once, let the silences hang: your customer will fill in the gaps with revealing information.

- *What would you like to have accomplished by the end of this engagement?*
- *Have you or your company ever engaged a company like ours?*
- *If so, how did it go? What went right? What would you like to see go better this time around?*
- *What are your budget expectations for this project?*
- *By when would you like the project completed?*
- *What issues, if any, do you foresee with the process we've laid out?*

Step 9. Understand the Personal

It's human nature to look for patterns. If your customer is a certain type of person in a certain type of company, you might typecast them. When you ask personal questions, however, you paint a picture of the obligations they face. These are different in every situation, and they impact expectations, especially the ones below the surface. Most importantly, personal questions help build the sort of relationship that is essential for repeat business. They allow you to turn your customer into your partner, which will compel them to be your advocate in relation to their company, just as you will be to them.

By "personal questions," I don't suggest asking about their home lives, but simply getting the sort of answers that start with "I" instead of the usual, business-like "we". Here are a few sample questions. Feel free to soften these with nurturing statements like, "if you don't mind me asking..."

- *What responsibilities are on you, personally, with this engagement?*
- *Just wondering, but what's your day-to-day like at your company?*
- *How will your success be measured?*

Step 10. Understand the Political

Don't worry, you won't be asking your customer who they voted for. After getting personal, the next step is understanding the relationship your customer has with their stakeholders, which will reveal the politics and culture of their organization. From there, you can anticipate new personalities entering the picture so you can manage expectations for the group as a whole. Here are some sample questions:

- *Who else will be involved with this project?*
- *What roles will they have?*
- *What is most important to them?*
- *Based on your experience, what should we do to make your team happy?*
- *What should we avoid doing?*
- *If you don't mind me asking, who are you most concerned about pleasing?*

Step 11. Put Out Fires by Offering Options

"Fires," or testy customer situations, might seem as varied as stars in the sky. When you diagnose the root cause, however, you find that most predicaments come from a failure to manage expectations.

When fires spark up, there's often a swerving tendency: account managers either get defensive and blame the customer, or they apologize profusely and blame everything on themselves and their team. It's best to get all parties back on the same page by conducting a reset call and revisiting expectations, perhaps by asking the earlier discovery questions. If the engagement is unsalvageable, find out what you should have done differently so you can prevent a similar situation in the future.

When it comes to fires, it helps if you can make your main contact your partner again. This means maintaining separate rapport from the one you have with the larger customer team. To do this, quiet yourself and listen to your customer's concerns, particularly the ways in which the fire made their life harder. From there, explain what your team did and why, and be **upfront** about your limitations and your own personal predicament. If you demonstrate that you are fighting for your partner, they will fight for you on their side.

It's tempting to get emotionally invested in a fire when customers make accusations and jabs. If tempers start to rise, recognize what's happening and take a pause. Get a second pair of eyes on touchy emails, preferably from someone who is uninvolved. Work toward improving the situation instead of falling into the trap of combativeness.

Most importantly, offer specific and tangible options. By offering options, you make it easier for everyone to move forward. Below is an effective email structure in response to a hypothetical fire.

Hi Customer,

Thanks for your candid feedback about the latest version of the hovercraft. I'm glad we had a chance to connect. I'm confident that we will create a product that exceeds your expectations.

We want to do everything we can to meet your needs, but including rocket boosters is beyond our ability for the timeframe and budget. Including the boosters would mean hiring on a specialist and asking our team to work significant overtime to meet the August 1st deadline. That being said, I'd like to lay out some options that might fit your needs:

- *A. We move the deadline to September 1st. This will allow us to add the boosters without additional charge.*
- *B. We levy overages of 25%, or $50,000, and we keep our current deadline. Given quality concerns in the face of the demanding timeline, we do not recommend this option.*
- *C. We use propellers instead of rocket boosters. Many of our previous customers have been pleased with this option, and we'd like to tell you more about it.*

I look forward to discussing these possibilities in greater detail. Can we plan on a conference call this week, say, tomorrow at 4 p.m.? If not, please let us know some times that work for you.

Best,
Account Manager

Step 12. Keep a Foibles List

Many consumer companies offer a frequently asked questions page, or an FAQ, to resolve the common issues their customers face. Though you will use it internally instead of externally, a foibles list serves a similar purpose by helping you identify common avoidable pitfalls. When fires arise, regardless of fault, jot down what happened, and include the date. I recommend keeping the list within your project management task list, and reviewing it before you start a new customer engagement. When you have repeated foibles, it probably means it's an area to be proactive about.

Step 13. Defer When You Have To

Many new account managers make the mistake of acquiescing to customer demands before consulting the people building the product. Though I usually huddled with my team about the big items, like final deadlines, it was the little stuff that started the fires. One fire starter, for example, was replying to a customer request with, "Sure, we can have 'X' for you by tomorrow morning!" Little did I realize that "X" meant taking an artist off of a more important project, and thus throwing a wrench in the gears.

To manage expectations, you have to understand your team's process and schedule. Unfortunately, maintaining this understanding in real time, and producing immediate answers for your customer is often impossible. When your customer requests something you can't promise before consulting your team, let them know you will have to get back to them.

This strategy is controversial. Some people question the purpose of an account manager if requests must be deferred. Although some might get annoyed, the alternative of sending customers to multiple stakeholders is much more aggravating for all parties. It's unreasonable to expect your customers to understand your company's structure and pass direction correctly (that's why your job exists).

Step 14. Keep Your Team Happy

Account management involves more than making the customer happy. You also have to keep up your team's morale. Though winning with the customer is priority, it's a draconian victory if you alienate your team in the process.

Though you will sometimes relay customer feedback to a larger group, when giving one-on-one direction use the medium that works best for each of your team members. If someone understands things better in email, then stick to that and use face-to-face or phone as a backup when further explanation is needed. Though this might take more time at the outset, it prevents revisions and backtracking.

When you talk in person with your peers, get on their level *literally*. All too often, there's a palpable disconnect, or even tension, because one person is hovering over the other. Hovering creates an atmosphere of hierarchy instead of collaboration. Communication is less encumbered when two people are at the same elevation.

Step 15. Question Deadlines

Will your customers have deadlines? Yes. Should you always do what you can to meet them? Of course. Do you have the right to ask questions about these deadlines? Absolutely.

If your customer gives you a deadline, don't respond, "Aye, aye!" Instead, ask why. Some deadlines are tough to get around, like those determined by events, but most are arbitrary. If the deadline is a serious crunch, emphasize that the timeframe will negatively impact quality. Submit a timeline detailing the demanding approval obligations expected of your customer. If necessary, let the customer know that you will have to charge a rush premium to bring on extra help (you can use the Adopt a Villain strategy discussed shortly on pg. 26). At this point, arbitrary deadlines tend to become quite flexible.

Step 16. Diagnose Missed Deadlines

When deadlines are missed, use them as learning experiences. Chances are, there's a bottleneck somewhere. First, figure out what was promised when, and see who is at fault, not for the purpose of casting blame, but so you can patch the leak. If your company is in remiss, figure out if (A) you, the account manager, outright over-promised, (B) someone on your team had trouble forecasting the amount of time it would take to complete a task, or (C) other obligations distracted your team from the deadline at hand.

Step 17. Provide a Timeline

Timelines are the cornerstone of expectation management, and you should submit one at the outset of every engagement. That being said, they invariably change, often at the customer's behest. With that in mind, use a timeline creator program that's intuitive and easy to edit. I've had the best experience with Tom's Planner.

You can learn more about Tom's Planner on the **Resources** page. Later we'll discuss how to use your timeline as a sales tool.

Step 18. Keep Up Momentum

I once led a broadcast commercial with an agency, which was liaison between us and the end client. When the agency middlemen presented our work to the client, they offered neither our recommendations nor ones of their own. It reminded me of over-courteous drivers approaching a four-way stop, everyone saying, "No, you go!" The unassertive behavior became endemic. The project dragged on forever as overwrought decisions replaced intuition.

This story taught me that less is more. Instead of giving your customer a multitude of options to choose from, give them two or three. Recommend the best one, even if you put it lightly. The customer may choose against your recommendation, but the simple act of suggesting something compels a decision. When you encourage swift but not hasty decisions, you produce better results than when you allow your customer to marinate on endless options.

While you must manage expectations, you also have to move your process along. Keeping momentum by making thoughtful recommendations allows your customer to rest easy knowing they hired an expert. After all, they're paying you to relieve the pain of decision making, not add to it.

Step 19. Adopt a Villain

In our company's dungeon lurked an elusive and enigmatic specter. Mentioning his name was too frightening, so he was referred to as "accounts receivable," or "our finance manager." Whenever something went wrong, the specter was blamed. One day he will have his revenge...

Sometimes, your customers will fall into remiss with respect to payments, feedback, or other obligations. Or maybe they will make demands before the start of an engagement that your company can't meet. When situations like these arise, it's handy to have someone who can take the heat so you can continue doing what you do best: being your customer's advocate and strengthening the relationship.

With that in mind, you should adopt a real or fictional colleague who can act as your villain. Maybe this is an accounts receivable "heavy" who enforces strict payment terms, or maybe it's a "legal department" who makes sure your contracts are enforced. Demonstrate that you are helping your customer navigate your company's policies and they will do the same for you.

Step 20. Be Clear and Firm About Your Process

From following these steps, eventually you will have constructed a finely-tuned machine for creating and/or implementing your offering. This machine will be built in a way that reflects your knowledge of what works and what doesn't. Some customers, however, will want you to build a custom machine just for them. In the trenches of a project, it's tempting to let them have their way. This is when you might find yourself working long into the night to give them things that aren't part of your normal process.

To avoid stress, be clear and firm about your process. Pre-identify areas where you're flexible and others where you can't budge. If customers start nudging you toward building a new machine, let them know that you will have to extend your time frame and budget. Whenever possible, end engagements with such problem customers. Their business probably isn't worth everything you're neglecting at their expense.

Step 21. Handle Unexpected Costs with Grace

The best way to handle objections in the face of overages and other unanticipated costs is to prevent surprises in the first place. To make things easy on yourself, include textual warnings about potential overages on the materials you submit to your customers. Before incurring overages, give customers the opportunity to change course.

That being said, your process won't always be linear. Despite warnings, misunderstandings, be they sincere or feigned, arise sometimes. Start by defusing tension. This doesn't come from waving around contracts or pointing fingers, it comes from explaining your situation. Here is a hypothetical email exchange:

Objection:

Hi Account Manager,

I'm not understanding what these overage charges are all about. At no point did we agree to these. I look forward to your response.

Best,
Customer

Response:

Hi Customer,

We originally contracted a custom website with 3 included design revisions. At this point, we have performed 5 revisions. As you will see on the cost breakdown, we are willing to waive one in good faith.

We do our best to communicate overages by noting them on each mockup. Also, overage details were noted in the contract and quote. I hope you appreciate that we could not stay in business if we kept on performing substantially more work than we are paid for.

Once you have the new site, we trust that it will deliver more value than it cost. I'm happy to speak with you to further clarify. Please let me know if that would be helpful.

Best,
Account Manager

The Account Management Dashboard (Steps 22-27)

I feel a serene calm pass over me as I gaze upon several gorgeous digital portals. What was yesterday a whirlwind of emails, mismatched contacts, and overlooked opportunities is now a dashboard, akin to that of a luxury sedan's, displaying accomplishments and attainable feats. How did I pull this off? By systematizing my customers and prospects into a few lists and charts, a task that took less than an hour.

That which seems impossible becomes easy when you organize it. These lists are the machinery you need to monitor progress in your mission of making strangers into customers, and customers into delighted customers.

Step 22. Create a Target List

Your Target List is where you organize the people you're pursuing. Your goals for them may differ depending on your role. Whether you're going after new business, product validation, press coverage from a media source, or something else, your Target List is where you keep your cold contacts, or those who do not know you.

Here is the information you should track: Company, Name, Title, Email, Phone, Dates Contacted, Next Steps.

Step 23. Create a Pipeline

Your Pipeline is where you keep your high potential prospects. These are people or companies with whom you have a rapport, and who are likely to buy or perform your desired action in the near future.

I've provided a sample Pipeline on the **Resources** page, which is formed by the below parameters. Feel free to copy it and use it yourself!

   A. **Likelihood:** the likelihood of sale or conversion from 10-100% (if less than 10%, your prospect shouldn't go in your Pipeline). You will determine what each 10% block represents by developing a Likelihood Legend that fits your product and sales process (more on this shortly).

B. **Estimated spend:** the dollar amount you estimate the prospect will be willing to invest, based on your conversations. If you're not dealing with a monetary situation, this might be a general value (i.e., a number from 1-100).

C. **Value:** Likelihood × Estimated Spend

D. **Date created:** the date the prospect entered your Pipeline.

E. **Last activity date:** columns D and E will help you determine how long your prospect has been in your Pipeline, and thus how the situation compares to your average sales cycle. If the length of time is longer than average, you might choose to lower the Likelihood.

F. **Next steps:** The next action you will take with the prospect.

Step 24. Develop Your Likelihood Legend

Predicting the likelihood of a prospect buying can be a shot in the dark. Some prospects I gave a 10% chance at buying, and they signed on with us the next day. Others I thought were in the bag, and I'd mark them at 90%, only to never hear from them again. The problem was that my criteria were arbitrary and inconsistent. That's when I was introduced to the Likelihood Legend.

Your Likelihood Legend accounts for most, if not all, of the sales situations you encounter, and each percentage reflects a certain status. To create each percentage status, review past sales situations with customers and prospects who didn't buy. Make sure to define how exactly a targeted prospect will enter your Pipeline to begin with. Often this means they express interest in further discussing your offering after you reach out via a cold call or email.

Here is my prototypical Likelihood Legend. It will work for many products and services. For convenience, you will find the legend as a note in the Pipeline found in **Resources**.

10%: Some potential

20%: Either (A) budget acceptable, or (B) firm time frame w/ unsure budget

40%: Budget acceptable and firm timeframe

50%: Budget acceptable, firm timeframe, start date is 2 weeks or less

60%: You're in the prospect's shortlist

75%: You're recommended to the ultimate decision maker

90%: Prospect *says* they're buying

100%: Contract signed (prospect leaves your Pipeline)

Step 25. Create a Farming List

This list is where you keep previous customers and prospects who have potential to move forward, but not in the near future. This is also known as your "tickler file." In a later section, we'll cover the ins and outs of farming and generating repeat business.

Information to track in your Farming List: company, name, title, email, phone, dates contacted, next steps.

Step 26. Create a Project Task List

The previous lists are designed to track progress toward a particular goal, which isn't always linear. A process-focused list makes sure recurring tasks are completed correctly every time. It's akin to a safety checklist filled out by an airline pilot, a fixture that makes air travel one of the safest transit methods.

As you communicate with your customers, write a one-sentence daily status line for each one. Make the status line prominent. By making yourself articulate your customer's status on a daily basis, you will always have a handle on what's going on. It might be, "Mayo Clinic: medical device set to be delivered on Monday," or "Davidson Restaurant Group: awaiting feedback on beta feature we presented last week."

Try using a checklist program, which will allow you to organize your projects, keep track of tasks, and be mindful of deadlines. My favorite is Asana (learn more about Asana in **Resources**).

Step 27. Forecast Revenue

At one point, in the midst of the day-to-day sales grind, I felt as though I couldn't see the forest for the trees. This coincided with our founder asking how accurately the Pipeline numbers were reflecting actual revenue. To get a look at the big picture, I began tracking the gross value of the Pipeline by recording the figures in a spreadsheet on a weekly basis.

This exercise was helpful for a few reasons. Tracking your forecasting accuracy tells you when you guessed right and when you missed the mark. This knowledge strengthens your ability to qualify prospects. Though it might take some time and experience to begin to forecast accurately, once you keep track of the total estimated value of your Pipeline, you can project future revenue.

The Sales Process (Steps 28-40)

I used to worry about coming off as a salesperson. I managed a complex, project-oriented product (animated explainer videos), and I didn't think there was a place for the clichéd hard-selling tactics that formed my myopic image of a salesperson. As a result, I failed to ask tough questions of my customers. Not only did this negatively affect my ability to understand their buying situation, it also left me in the dark about their needs once they purchased from us.

I soon learned there was much more to sales than antiquated gimmicks and hard selling. I wrote and started using a sales script. Though it took some practice, before long I began closing more deals. More importantly, I started new customer engagements with a complete understanding of needs. Projects went more smoothly, and our customers left happier.

Regardless of whether or not your day-to-day involves working to close new business, developing a sales process will make you a stronger account manager, and it will be helpful in all sorts of personal and professional situations.

The goal of your first call or meeting will be to qualify your prospect. This means learning about their problems and goals, budget situation, start and finish dates, and decision-making process, among other things. It's like the Who, What, Where, When, Why, and How. In the following steps, we'll cover the qualification points you should narrow down. You will find re-purposable questions that formed a script I used to qualify many prospects. Some of these concepts are interpolated from the Serving Your Customers section. This is so you can contextualize them for sales and organize them within a script. Using a script is a winning strategy because it allows you to guide the conversation. If you don't guide the conversation, your prospect will, and you probably won't be able to qualify them.

Although order is important, your script is meant to give you flexibility. You can envision it as a library of questions and statements. Once you internalize this library, you can shift things around in response to the situation.

Step 28. Start Conversations the Right Way

Make sure your prospect is on the same page when it comes to expectations. Keep in mind that you will be asking tough questions, and your prospect should be prepared for them. Start by getting permission to conduct an interview.

- *I'd like to ask you some questions to learn more about your needs. From there, I'll be able to tell you about our process and price. By the end of our call, I should have an accurate estimate for you, and we'll have a chance to discuss what would make sense as the best next step. Does that work for you?*

Nothing will throw you off more than getting to the middle of your conversation and finding out your prospect has to jump off in two minutes. With that in mind, at the start, make a point of finding out how much time you have. If less than desirable, reschedule or re-prioritize your questions.

- *We will need about 15 minutes. Does that work for you?*

Step 29. Enjoy the Silence

When you ask tough questions, sometimes you will face disconcerting silences. When this happens, take a deep breath, and let your inquiries hang. When you don't fill the air, your prospect will, and the gems they reveal will enlighten you.

Step 30. Uncover Problems

70% of people make purchasing decisions to solve problems, and only 30% make decisions to gain something (source: Impact Communications). With that in mind, the core of your sales conversations should center on uncovering problems.

Before I understood how to find problems, I was befuddled when deals fizzled out. Prospects were into our product, and our price was generally agreeable, but then I got unresponsiveness and delays at the eleventh hour: "We're waiting for our new CMO to get onboard", "We've been very busy with other projects", "Our company dog is sick. " In these situations, the problems weren't big enough to justify change. After learning how to uncover problems, I was able to compel buying decisions, or at least get the time wasters out of my life.

The problems you unveil in your first meeting with your customer will carry throughout the relationship. Your early understanding of their needs will allow you to anticipate and manage their expectations, and communicate them to the rest of your team.

Here are some sample questions for uncovering problems:

- *Would you mind giving me a high-level overview of your business?*
- *Why are you interested in our product?*
- *Who are you targeting with your marketing efforts?*
- *What has your strategy been up until now? What impact has it had?*
- *If you don't mind me asking, what is your average deal size?*
- *Is that a big purchase for your customers? How long is the sales cycle?*

- *What concepts have been difficult to explain that you might want to focus on?*
- *Just wondering, but what sort of obligations are on you, personally, with this project?*
- *What's important to you, personally, in regard to selecting a provider?*

Step 31. Find Previous Industry Experience

Continuing from the last step, the below questions uncover problems by finding out about your prospect's experience in your industry. If your prospect does have experience, they will probably have specific expectations. If they don't, then they will probably have concerns about your industry in general. Get to these inquires early because they will inform the rest of your conversation.

- *Has your company ever worked with a company like ours?*
- *What was that experience like?*
- *Based on your past experience, what would you like to see go right?*
- *What outcomes would you like to avoid?*

Step 32. Identify Goals

Asking your prospect to identify goals is another method for uncovering problems. By asking your prospect to identify what they want for the future, they usually tell you how present conditions should change.

- *What would you like our offering to accomplish?*
- *What should the product do in order for you to consider it a success?*
- *How will you measure the success of this engagement?*
- *What sort of positive reception would you need in order to consider the product worth the investment?*
- *This is always a tough question, but how many leads/positive reviews/revenue/etc. would our offering need to bring in for you to consider it a success?*

Goal-related questions are tough, and sometimes they are met with befuddlement. When this happens, put numbers on the blank page and it will be easier to get answers:

- *Hypothetically, if our offering generated five new leads every month, would that be successful?*
- *If the product increased employee awareness of the topics you mentioned by 20%, would that be a win?*

Step 33. Pad Your Questions

Make sure your prospect feels that they are undergoing a consultation and not an interrogation. You can take the heat off by softening your statements. The best padding statements present position your questions to your prospect's benefit.

- *Thanks for bearing with me on these questions. These details help me figure out what would be the best fit for your needs.*
- *To see if our offering is the right fit, would you please tell me…*
- *Just wondering…*
- *If you don't mind me asking…*
- *Just curious…*
- *Would you mind telling me…*

Step 34. Uncover Budget

Now that you have dug into your prospect's problems, it's time to figure out if they can afford you. Uncovering budget involves more than simply presenting your price and asking if it's agreeable. Instead, learn about your prospect's goals as they apply to their budget.

The below questions pick up where the goal-related inquiries left off. Since talking about the numbers might be a little uncomfortable, remember to make nurturing statements. From this line of questioning, you will start to paint a picture of your prospect's budget situation.

If you find yourself getting pushed toward giving your price before you're ready, let the prospect know that an accurate quote will require narrowing down more details.

A caveat: If the prospect asks twice for a price (or other information), give it to them. Holding out after the second ask creates aggravation. You can give a rough estimate to keep the conversation open.

- ACCOUNT MANAGER: "Earlier you mentioned that ideally you want the campaign to generate five new leads per month. Just wondering, what's your close rate?"
- PROSPECT: "Around 10%."
- AM: "You mentioned that your average deal is $200,000. Just so I understand, it sounds like your target monthly revenue for the campaign, based on your 10% close rate, would be around $400,000. Does that sound right to you?"
- P: "Yes, that's about right."
- AM: "Excellent. I think we'll be a good fit then."

Step 35. Present Your Price & Keep the Conversation Open

For now, frame your price in a way that continues the conversation. If you get a positive response, don't stop digging. Some prospects won't be truthful about budget because they know that if they say they can't afford you, the free consulting will end. Others might feel awkward about shutting down a pleasant conversation in the face of monetary differences. A third group is too low on the totem pole to know what budget they're working with.

- *Based on our discussion and my experience, my initial recommendation is a standard widget at $12,000-$14,000, depending on the approach we take. How does that resonate with you?*

- *I'm just wondering, but what similar investments are you making in this area?*
- *Just to double-check that I'm not wasting your time, is our price generally in line?*

Price objections will happen. In the next section you will find methods for responding to them, and exploring all budget opportunities.

Step 36. Find Start & Finish Dates

The below questions are designed to pinpoint when your prospect wants to get started and be finished. Finding the time frame is important because you need to make sure your prospect has immediate plans, and not a distant pipedreams. Those with the latter will waste your time.

> *By when would you like to have the project done?*
> *By when do you want to get started?*
> *By when would you like to select a provider?*

In the next section, you will learn methods for responding to time frame objections, and tying prospects to the calendar.

Step 37. Make Your Pitch - Focus on the "Why"

Eventually you will have to discuss your offering, or give your pitch. This is the information your prospect is hankering for. Have you ever felt like your audience is mentally shuffling out of the room when you start talking about yourself or your offering? You might feel like their bodies are still there, but their minds are elsewhere. This is usually when the phones come out.... I had this uneasy feeling as I rattled off about the "features" and "benefits" of our videos. After receiving constructive criticism, I rewrote my pitch to focus on why it is we do what we do. This involved a straightforward opener:

"We started our company because we realized that your audience needs to understand your message quickly, but more importantly, they must remember it."

Once I centered my spiel on the "why," I felt an immediate emotional connection with my audience. Whether I won the business or not, it became clear that my prospects knew that we were different, and that they would remember us. The *why* is your mission, and it's your most powerful differentiator. Build your pitch around it.

Once you cover the "why", focus on the specific ways in which you are different. Many pitches stop there, but it's important bring it all home for your audience by talking about why these difference matter.

I suggest giving your pitch before launching into the next round of questions about the decision-making process. By breaking from your questions to offer information, you maintain a conversation and not an interrogation. Since it's somewhat obvious that the next round of questions are asked for your benefit, throwing the prospect a bone at this stage makes getting answers much easier.

Step 38. Get to the Decision Maker

The goal here is to get in front of the decision maker. If that's not possible, get an understanding of your prospect's decision-making process, which means figuring out who decides and how. In a typical firm with 100-500 employees, an average of 7 people are involved in most buying decisions (source: Gartner Group).

Since you're doing a bit of prying, throw out nurturing statements like candy, and *never* ask the demeaning question, "Who is the decision maker?"

Here are some good questions for uncovering your prospect's decision-making process. As per most great inquiries, they're open-ended.

- *How is a decision like this typically made?*
- *What will be the main factors guiding your decision?*
- *After you're done talking with me and the other vendors you're considering, what happens next?*
- *Will you be recommending a particular provider to your superiors?*
- *How will you decide who your recommended provider is?*
- *What can we do to become your recommendation?*

Step 39. Get a Follow Up Appointment

It was another hopeless end to an otherwise promising first call. The prospect said he would get back to me after speaking with his team. That's when the mental straw-grasping started because experience told me that his response was doubtful. This time, instead of floundering, I asked questions like the ones you will find below.

In response, I got answers informing me about his decision-making process, and a "yes" to my request for a meeting. My continued involvement made us a shoo-in, and we landed the business.

Getting a follow up appointment is vital - 80% of potential opportunities are lost without trace simply due to lack of follow-up (source: Robert Clay). Your prospects will often present the findings from your first conversation to a larger group. When this happens, offer to relieve the hassle of reiteration by joining them during their meeting. As we will talk about later, during your second conversation, you can present tools and insights that help your prospects make an informed decision. There are tons of ways to offer value and continue rapport.

As you continue the conversation, make sure you understand the buying situation. Situations evolve, and prospects won't always communicate these changes.

- *What materials would be helpful for you to have on hand before your meeting?*
- *What are the next steps after you speak with your team?*
- *We covered a lot of ground on our call, and I know details can get lost in translation. With that in mind, would it be helpful if I joined you and your team during the meeting so you don't have to reiterate?*
- *Please expect my call next week to discuss best next steps.*

Step 40. Close by Defining What Closing Means

Traditional sales literature espouses all sorts of crafty techniques for tipping prospects over the edge into customer-dom. One of the more memorable ruses is the "assumptive close", where you play dumb and assume that the prospect is ready to purchase, asking, "What time should I schedule the delivery?"

These gimmicks don't work, and they seem to persist because of salespeople applying causation to correlation. Closing is simply the last logical step in your goal-oriented conversations.

That being said, a common barrier to closing happens when prospects don't know what steps they need to take to become customers. With complex offerings, it's not always clear when consulting ends and engagement begins. The straightforward act of communicating the action required to get started will dramatically improve, or at least speed up, the way you close.

- *To get started, we would need signoff on our services agreement and an engagement payment of 50%. With that in mind, what are the best next steps for you on this project?*

Responding to Objections (Steps 41-49)

I named this section "Responding to Objections" and not "Handling Objections" because not everyone is the right fit for your offering. Admitting this is a lot more powerful than arguing and fast-talking in the face of objections. Accepting that you might not be the right fit takes the pressure off. To the prospect, you become a consultant and not a salesperson. This atmosphere allows you to have a casual discussion about the prospect's needs. From there, you can explore every possibility to make something work.

Step 41. Handle Competitors by Facing Them Head-on

Instead of pretending like competition doesn't exist, encourage your prospect to stack you up against your competitors. Give them helpful tools so they can make an objective comparison, but make sure the materials accentuate your strengths. One possibility is a comparison chart, which we'll talk about in the Tools and Tips section.

Step 42. Explore All Budget Possibilities

Although not everyone will be a fit for your product, it's important to explore all possibilities when price objections come up. Once you have a read on your prospect's target budget, you might be able to offer a lower-cost alternative. When you do this, admit that you are trying to fit your offering to your prospect's needs so they can have all the options; otherwise, it sounds like you're reconnoitering yourself against their best interests.

If the budget is truly untenable, then send your prospect to a lower-cost provider from whom you receive a commission. Remember to sell your partner a bit, and emphasize that you're recommending the best value you've seen at their price range. If this isn't an option, recommend a solution that will fit their needs.

- *Thanks for your candor. I'd still like to see how I can help out, maybe by making the right recommendation. Do you mind me asking what general budget you're aiming for?*
- *Thanks for letting me know what you're aiming for. For your budget of $10,000 I think a 1-minute video might be a good fit. We often find that longer videos don't necessarily equal better videos because they experience high drop-off rates. Also, shorter videos tend to get shared more. As you can*

probably tell, I'm trying to see how our capabilities might fit your budget. I just want to make sure you have all the options. Is a 1-minute video something you might entertain?

- *Considering your target budget, I don't think we would be the best fit. I often send people to XYZ provider, and I think they will provide the best value at your price range. Would it be helpful if I introduced you?*

Step 43. Use Delays to Create Urgency

When a prospect delays getting started, find out if the delay is serious by asking the first question below. Once you know the delay is real and not an excuse, provide a timeline detailing how long it will take to get your prospect set up (i.e., contracts, payment, etc.), and how long it will take to implement your product. When people are juggling different projects and schedules, they often have trouble conceptualizing how long things take. If your prospect is indeed serious, walking them through your timeline will create a sense of urgency.

If the delay sounds like an excuse, "go for the no" via the second question. Though a "yes" is the best, a "no" boots out the time-wasters.

- *Thanks for the update. I'm just wondering, what will be different at that time?*
- *In my experience, such delays are often a polite way of saying "no," which would be no big deal! I'm just wondering, is that the case here?*

Step 44. End Unresponsiveness

Unresponsive prospects steal your attention from more promising opportunities. When it comes to getting responses, the below template is the most effective I've ever tried. Don't question it, just use it. We'll analyze why it works next.

> Hi,
> You're probably quite busy, or somehow my last email didn't reach you, so I thought I'd reach out again and check in as to where we are with the project.
>
> I'm sure you realize that I'm being professionally persistent, but if you are not interested or things have changed, I would appreciate you letting me know so we can determine what the best next step should be.
>
> Look forward to your thoughts.
>
> Best,
> Account Manager

This email is powerful because it admits that you're at fault. Instead of skirting the issue and pretending that you're not acting like a salesperson, you come right out and say it.

"Professionally persistent" is a useful little phrase. It contextualizes your intrusions. It turns you from a pest into a professional.

If unresponsiveness continues after this email, let the recipient know that you're closing the file. This often appeals to their loss aversion by letting them know that an opportunity is about to pass them by.

Hi,

Since I've had some trouble getting in touch with you, should I assume that either the project is on hold or that you have gone in another direction?

I thought I'd check back once more before I close the file on this for now. Please let me know whether or not it would be purposeful to continue the conversation. If not, hopefully we'll get the chance to work together in the future.

Best,
Account Manager

Step 45. Handle Pre-Conversation Price Requests

When shopping for a complex offering, most people will be willing to have a conversation. That said, there is an ever-present contingent that demands a price before having a conversation. When this happens, try a response like the one in the following scenario.

Most serious prospects will agree to a conversation once you make the point that it's in their best interest. If they continue to insist on a price, give them a very rough ballpark, remove them from your Pipeline, and move on. If they're not serious enough to pick up the phone, they're probably not worth your time.

Prospect:

Hi,

Would you please provide me with rough pricing on a widget of XYZ specs?

Thanks,
Prospect

Account Manager:

Hi,

I can give a very rough ballpark, but in my experience, these numbers aren't very accurate until I understand needs. After learning more, I should be able to give you an accurate quote, and more information on our process and timeframe. With that in mind, can we plan on connecting briefly at 3 p.m. ET? If not, please let me know some times that work for you.

Best,
Account Manager

Step 46. Make Negotiations Matter

Negotiating, when done right, is valuable because it lets you explore every opportunity to make something work. Typically, your prospect will want to negotiate when you're a shortlisted provider, or the chosen one. Sometimes they will tell you upfront what budget they are aiming for, but usually they will start by asking if you can go lower. When this happens, ask what price they need to make a commitment.

Even if you have the authority to decide whether or not you will lower your price, pretend that you do not. You have more leverage as a subordinate. Deferring power to a real or mythical decision maker allows you to be the good guy in the negotiation. Instead of acting as the roadblock, you fill the role of the hero who wants everything to work out. This role will persist when your prospect becomes your customer (this is the pre-purchase version of the "Adopt a Villain" (pg. 26) technique discussed earlier).

Continue the negotiation by asking your prospect to define their "must-haves" and their "nice-to-haves." Only concede when you can get something in return; otherwise, it makes your pricing seem arbitrary.

- *What price would you need in order to move forward?*
- *To avoid wasting each other's time, I'd like to make sure we are the right fit before I go to my management to get approval on a discount. My team won't be able to suggest the*

best possible option until they know what you are aiming for.

- *Because I'm sure our finance manager will ask me, would you entertain faster payment terms if I'm able to get approval on a discount?*

Step 47. Get Paid on Time

It's a childish game companies play with respect to when they pay each other. Many organizations maintain terms of "net 45" or longer, which means they essentially demand short-term loans from their vendors. In the excitement of a closed deal, I often forgot to inquire about payment terms, which left us waiting for payment months after projects ended.

Your payment terms conversation should happen during the negotiation phase, not after it. If the terms are longer than desirable, get permission to invoice early so you will be paid in a timely manner.

Most medium and large organizations use an accounts payable department (AP). Your goal should be to deal directly with AP so you don't strain your relationship with your main customer contact over petty money matters. That being said, you want your main customer on hand to nudge AP when they drag their feet.

If your customer is seriously late, don't be afraid to withhold delivery of assets. You can blame your villain, letting your main contact know that you're working on their behalf to work through your company's payment policies.

Step 48. Know How to Lose a Deal Successfully

Though losing sucks, it's a great opportunity to learn. When you win business, you rarely scrutinize the situation to pinpoint what you did right. The high of success clouds critical thinking. This might be a dumbly obvious point, but once you have lost you have nothing to lose. When this happens, ask your prospect questions to gain as much insight as possible. Be persistent to get answers, and follow up when further explanation is warranted. As always, keep your questions open-ended.

- *What was the main factor driving your decision?*
- *I hope you don't mind me asking, but what provider did you choose?*
- *Just wondering, but what general budget did you settle on?*
- *What should I have done differently?*

Step 49. Take Off Your Sales Hat

In some situations, your prospect will be ambivalent about their decision, or perhaps they are testing the waters with another company before making a weightier decision. In such cases, make clear that you accept their choice. Set up a quick "debrief" call for the purposes of (A) making sure their solution is properly implemented, and (B) learning how you can better meet the needs of their industry in the future. Take the pressure off, come with helpful information in-hand, and use the opportunity to learn new details about their buying situation. With this approach, you can explore opportunities to do business in the future, and sometimes you can pull lost deals back from the abyss by introducing new considerations. You have nothing to lose!

Tips and Tools
(Steps 50-63)

Another signature took shape on the dotted line, this time from a Fortune 500 equipment and software distributor. The project involved creating a video up-selling their new database product to their existing customers. I was surprised that the deal worked out because the customer was very price-sensitive, and our offering is on the higher end. After reflecting on the whole sales process, I realized how I landed it: I shifted the conversation from a focus on price to quality by providing a comparison chart focused on the latter. After showing my prospect how to compare quality with this tool, she began to change her priorities. Eventually, the quality argument won us the job, and expectations were exceeded.

Now that you are developing your sales script and staying ahead of common objections, it's time to build your tool belt. Your tool belt will include materials that will shift your prospect's decision-making process in your favor. As mentioned earlier, I keep a list of new and timeless tools in **Resources**.

Additionally, this section is as good as any for imparting general tips and advice for becoming a better, faster, stronger account manager.

Step 50. Use a Competitive Comparison Chart

To elaborate on the above, a competitive comparison chart is a spreadsheet with the parameters for comparing your product to a competitor's. Ideally, it lists parameters that the layperson wouldn't think to consider. For example, our animated video comparison chart encourages prospects to compare sound effects and voice-over recording quality, among other areas. A comparison chart works well because it assists in the decision-making process, while influencing the prospect to choose you. As such, you can use the chart to accentuate your strengths over the competition. If you're the discount provider, incorporate price into the chart. If you're the high-end provider, focus on quality and take price out of the equation.

Step 51. Use an ROI Calculator

Most salespeople use promotional tools. Though they have their place, offering value is much more effective. You should provide tools that will be helpful to your prospect whether they ultimately buy from you or a competitor. An ROI calculator is one such tool, and it typically consists of a spreadsheet with instructions.

Depending on your product, ROI might mean dollars, or another metric like viewer engagement, positive feedback, or decrease in workplace accidents. Later, we will talk about incorporating this into a take-home guide for farming future business with your customers.

Step 52. Offer Curated Case Studies

The success of a case study is all about curation, and often less is more. Salespeople tend to overwhelm their prospects with massive case study decks. The lengthiness of a deck makes the prospect unlikely to read much of it. If they do read it, they will probably see it for what it is: a mound of canned sales collateral.

Instead give prospects the impression that you put thought into their situation, and perused a library of case studies to find the most relevant ones. This strategy makes all the more sense when you don't have many from which to choose.

Step 53. Bring Prospects Back to Reality with a Timeline

As discussed earlier, timing-based objections can either be a sign that the problem is too small, or they can be legitimate excuses. When the latter is the case, a timeline will bring prospects back to reality by visually depicting how long it will take to get set up and implement your offering. Also, a timeline sets expectations early on. This helps move the sales process forward, and it puts you a step ahead when it comes to managing the project.

Step 54. Use Visuals

Since your prospect is probably comparing providers, your offering is competing for mental real estate. Your prospect is juggling lots of details and keeping up with the usual barrage or workday information stimulus. With that in mind, it's important to keep your offering from getting lost in the noise. To create a lasting impression, share memorable visual references. After all, visuals are processed 60,000x faster than text (source: Neo Mammalian Studios). These visuals might be related to your product or industry as a whole. Again, make sure they offer value regardless of your prospect's ultimate decision.

Step 55. Get Warmed Up to Sell

Before you go for a long run, you start by stretching. Your stretches last only a few minutes, and in no time you're up and moving. The real warm up starts as you jog. You get acclimated to the exercise through the exercise itself.

Using your verbal and cognitive skills to sell is a similar process: you have to warm yourself up through the exercise of a goal-oriented conversation. Often account managers waste too much time "stretching." They avoid the discomfort of talking to strangers by procrastinating with emails and busy work.

To get ready for a day of sales conversations, get yourself on the phone with a prospect within ten minutes of arriving at your desk (it doesn't matter if the prospect is unqualified). When you acclimate yourself to the discomfort of a sales call or meeting, the rest of your daily conversations will flow comfortably and naturally. Also, it's easier to avoid gatekeepers and answering machines when you call bright and early.

Step 56. Stand Up

One day while lounging in my comfy office chair, I read an article about how sitting is killing me. It scared the bejeezus out of me, so I bought a standing desk on Amazon and started working on my feet. Suffice to say, fear was my motivator. It's certainly a good one, but it's not the only one to consider....

The benefits of working while standing up are extensive. This relatively small action will positively transform your life. In addition to giving you more energy, standing opens up your diaphragm and allows you to speak more clearly and effortlessly. This is why you don't usually find rock vocalists and opera singers sitting on office chairs when they perform.

Furthermore, standing is an authoritative position, and your body language affects your emotional state. Reciprocally, your posture affects the ways in which others perceive you (source: Amy Cuddy). With that in mind, living life on your feet can improve confidence in subtle but powerful ways. This advantage is invaluable when you're having difficult conversations with prospects and customers.

To get started, make sure you have a decent standing desk. There are plenty of great options out there. Also, pick up a corrective mat, which will take a lot of the strain off of your feet and lower back (my favorite desk and mat are included in **Resources**). Give it a try for a week, and keep at it from morning until 4 p.m., excluding a break for lunch. Once you temper your underused leg muscles, it's smooth sailing.

Step 57. Use Your Experience

In our digital age, everyone can pretend to be an expert. Your prospect might conduct a few minutes of research, and they think they understand your industry. If you argue with their assumptions, they will feel like they're being sold, and they will back away. No matter how honest or helpful you're trying to be, the perception is that you're blowing smoke.

Your recommendations will be taken seriously when you unleash the power of "your experience." While prospects can argue with your biased claims, it's nearly impossible to argue with your experience. On the contrary, you can almost hear ears perking up when you start a sentence with, "In my experience..." The phrase sounds humble and it builds a conversation instead of an argument. The prospect thinks, "I'm about to get free consulting, and I better lap up as much as I can."

Step 58. Write Your Prospects' RFPs

I've landed the biggest deals of my career through Requests for Proposals, or RFPs. I've also squandered a lot of time completing them for those who would never buy. The next few steps will talk about how to win the lucrative engagements extended through RFPs.

Many RFP's fail to accurately reflect the product or industry they're addressing. Many use the wrong jargon, ill-fitting pricing schemes, or they emphasize irrelevant criteria. The prospect's ignorance of your industry allows you the opportunity to help them write the RFP. When you're able to speak with your prospect before they blast out the RFP, offer up your experience to ensure that their request hits the mark. Your collaboration will be the foundation for a relationship, and you can stack the cards in your favor by making the RFP emphasize the areas in which your company excels.

Step 59. Do Proposals for the Well-Qualified

Proposals require a big time investment, and you should only do them for well-qualified prospects. When you receive an RFP, go through your normal sales process, as discussed earlier. After talking about price, or at least providing a general ballpark, ask flat out if completing a proposal would be worth your time. I've received surprisingly candid and revealing responses. RFP submitters are often bound to bureaucratic rules, and sometimes they resist phone or in-person conversations. At the end of the day, if you can't get a conversation, it's not worth doing the proposal.

- *I read through the proposal, but I have some questions that will be easiest to discuss on the phone. To make sure I provide the most accurate details about our process and price, I'd like to have a brief conversation about your needs. Can we talk tomorrow at 3 p.m. ET? If not, please let me know some times that work for you.*
- *In my experience, proposals like yours require a day's work from me and my team. Before we invest that time, I'd like to make sure our offering is generally in line with what you're aiming for. An offering like the one discussed would be $20,000-$25,000. With that in mind, would it be purposeful for us to submit a proposal?*

Step 60. Follow Proposal Directions

Once you decide that a proposal is worth your time, make sure you provide the requested information in the specific order assigned. RFPs are designed to be scientific: though you can inject your style and differentiators, avoid breaking the RFP's conventions.

Keep up the conversation before, during, and after submitting your proposal. Arrange a follow-up call immediately before submitting to make sure everything is clear. Let your prospect know that regardless of the outcome, you will be following up to discuss the results.

Step 61. Qualify Prospects Before They Talk to Your Team

Sometimes prospects will ask to speak to someone above you on the totem pole or to your colleagues who create or implement your offering. They might think that a specialist will give them better insight, or that removing the middleman will put them in a better negotiating position.

Setting up a call with a superior or colleague can be an effective strategy in some situations. A conversation between like-minded professionals can help build a relationship and move the buying process along. Owners enjoy speaking with owners, and same in respect to designers, developers, mechanics, and other specialists.

That being said, you don't want to waste your team's time on those who are not serious. First, learn about your prospect's goals, and go through your normal sales process. Make sure to ask questions like the one below before hooking them up with your team. If they answer with vagaries or you get the gut feeling that you're dealing with a time-waster, apologize and let them know that your team is bogged down at the moment.

- *What would you like to have accomplished by the end of the conversation with my superior/colleague?*

Step 62. Prevent Sales Atrophy

One of your biggest challenges will be keeping your head in the game. This means continually qualifying prospects and being persistent. When laziness and self-doubt creep up, you have to recognize these thoughts for what they are: head trash. When you identify the hazards, you can overcome them when they arise.

After speaking with dozens of prospects who have similar apparent needs, you might begin to make assumptions about their ability to buy. This is dangerous because it leads you to fall back on old habits, and then you miss opportunities. You might be tempted to let yourself fall into the prospect's interview process because it's comfortable. You might make the lazy choice to write an email instead of picking up the phone, causing you to miss revealing details that will only be communicated over voice. You might not push for a follow-up call because you fear coming off as a pest. You might start to feel like a broken record repeating the same questions over and over.

Although your process might feel repetitive to you, it's new to your prospect, and they won't share your doubts. When you feel yourself slipping, review your script and stick to it.

Step 63. Work Remotely

To give credit where it's due, my interest and general method for pursuing a remote work arrangement was first inspired by Tim Ferriss' approach in *The Four Hour Work Week*. That said, I wanted to offer some specifics for account managers. More than other professions, account managers have to deal with a ton of distractions. Since you have an internal boss and a gang of external bosses (your customers), you face constant requests for meetings, conference calls, and email responses; not to mention run-of-the-mill office diversions like noisiness, interjections, and commuting. This atmosphere often makes mountains out of molehills. Inconsequential customer emails demand immediate response at the perceived risk of losing the account. The ongoing fire drill makes it difficult to batch your tasks and maintain effective sales and customer services processes. When everything is needed ASAP, nothing truly is, and everyone suffers, especially your customers.

A remote work arrangement will give you the autonomy to maintain your own processes and serve your customers better. When you don't have to answer every email immediately, you will get things done.

Before approaching your boss about a remote work arrangement, take a remote work "sick day." When you return, find an ideal time to speak with your boss and explain how working remotely allowed you to serve your customers better. Propose testing out a remote work arrangement on Fridays. If it doesn't go well, your boss can always end it. If you face objections, acknowledge them respectfully to avoid a self-defeating argument.

Here are some common objections against working remotely, and ways to handle them:

- Technology Hurdles
  Objection Statement: *"How will you deal with inbound sales calls? How will you access files? How will you communicate with us?"*
  How to Handle: Research remote solutions, and talk about them during your meeting. These might include VoIP services for handling call forwarding, Dropbox or SpiderOak for file sharing, and Skype for teleconferencing.

- Bandwagoning
  Objection Statement: *"If I let you do it, then I'll have to let everyone do it."*
  How to Handle: Remind your boss that you're proposing a test. If others can demonstrate their effectiveness, then perhaps the arrangement is worth considering for them as well. Alternatively, and this is a bit touchier, you can suggest that your boss reject similar requests by telling employees that you're dealing with "personal issues."

- Need for Face-to-Face

  Objection Statement: *"Collaboration is easier when every-one is in the same space."*

  How to Handle: Acknowledge that this can be true, but emphasize the flip side: the office environment is rife with distractions. Emphasize the office's downsides without pinning anything on your boss or coworkers. In fact, mention that you find yourself more likely to reflexively ask unnecessary questions and distract your peers when you're in an office environment. When you're working remotely, you are more likely to consider the question carefully and look for answers before bringing it to another's attention. Make the case that though face-to-face collaboration can be helpful, you find that you get more done in a self-guided, solo environment.

Once you have demonstrated remote effectiveness for some time, see if you can get approval to experiment with an additional day.

Farming
(Steps 64-73)

In the face of long and exhausting projects, at completion I often sent customers on their merry way. I invoiced, delivered the files, and said goodbye. There was a better way to do things....

After looking at the numbers, I found that repeat business represented over 50% of our revenue, so I began to push for more repeat jobs and referrals.

I had collegial relationships with many of my customers, which, at face value, might make the task of getting repeat business seem straightforward. Instead, I found it particularly awkward asking my customers to reopen their wallets or send us to their friends who would. After marinating on the problem and trying different things, I started being upfront about my situation. I'd say, "This is kinda uncomfortable for me, but as a good sales guy I'd be remiss if I didn't ask for referrals. With that in mind, I'm wondering, who in your world would be a good fit for our services?" Once I was transparent, most of my customers were helpful, and I reaped the rewards.

At the end of a successful engagement, the post-coital afterglow of the finish line is the perfect atmosphere for generating future rewards, which go beyond just revenue. You will be farming with pride in no time!

Step 64. Conduct a Debrief Call

Not enough account managers make a point of saying "bon voyage" to their customers after an engagement. They get swamped with other things, so they let customers shuffle out with a cursory "nice workin' with ya" email. Break from the pack by conducting a "debrief" meeting or call at the end of every engagement. The debrief is a golden opportunity to gain referrals, repeat business, and other benefits.

Your wrap-up email (below) sets the stage for the debrief. The important thing is to counterbalance the value your customer expects you to request (referrals or future business) with the value you offer (helpful information).

Hi Customer,

It's been a pleasure working with you. We hope the product serves you well!

I wanted to have a quick "debrief" call to learn about your overall experience with us. Also, I'd like to see what recommendations I can make for implementing and using the product.

I've attached our Take-Home Guide, which I think will be helpful. I look forward to explaining it in detail.

Can we plan on connecting on Wednesday at 2 p.m. ? If not, please let me know some times that work. We will need around 15 minutes.

Best,
Account Manager

Step 65. Get Honest Feedback

Too often, account managers neglect asking tough questions to find out where they stand with their customers. Before you start asking for repeat business, referrals, and other gifts, it's vital to get a barometer on your customer's experience. This information will let you know if they are ready to help you, or if you first need to repair the relationship. Also, asking your customer to take a jab at you has the psychological effect of compelling them to soften the blow, perhaps by fulfilling your future requests.

- *What was your experience with us like?*
- *What did we do right throughout the process?*
- *Where did we fall short?*
- *What can we do better next time?*

Step 66. Find Repeat Biz Opportunities

Repeat business usually hinges on the success of the first engagement. From your customer's perspective, success may depend heavily on the performance of the product over time. With that in mind, the best way to ensure your customer's satisfaction and secure their repeat business is to keep in touch with them. Stay up to speed on their results, and offer resources or support to ensure their success. One way to stay abreast of things is to partner with your customer to create a case study, which we'll discuss shortly.

When a customer is happy with you and your offering, they will find an excuse to work with you again. First, however, you have to be upfront about your intentions and start a conversation about future opportunities. The below sample questions will start that conversation. Try incorporating them into your debrief.

- *What are your plans for the product?*
- *When might be a good time to get back in touch about the impact of the product?*

- *What opportunities do you foresee to work together again in the future?*
- *What can we do to work with you again?*
- *In what situations would you envision working together in the future?*

Step 67. Ask for Referrals

Referrals can become your #1 revenue source, but first you have to ask for them. It's best to ask at the beginning and end of the engagement because those are the times when your customer is most excited about your offering. As for phrasing, go for open-ended questions like these:

- *I'm wondering, who in your world might benefit from our services?*
- *What other departments in your organization might benefit from our services? Would you mind putting us in touch?*
- *Not to put you on the spot, but after our call, would you mind introducing me to one or two people who you think might benefit from our offering?*

Step 68. Be Persistent

Send one or two polite follow-ups as needed to get referrals. Make the referral intros convenient and casual for your customer. If they're having trouble thinking of them, reduce the size of your ask and request that they send you to just one friend who would benefit from your offering. On Sidekick by Hubspot, Steli Efti recommends this process: ask for the referral; anticipate a "no" and ask one more time; make things easy for your customer by providing them an email template to use, like this one:

Hi Customer,

I wanted to introduce you to Dan, his company does XYZ. I think this will be interesting for you, and I think you will both have a fruitful conversation.

I'll let you guys take it from here.

Best,
Account Manager

Step 69. Get Marketing Advice

When new customers purchase from you, it's a great strategy to ask, "How did you find us?" The collective answers let you know what marketing channels are performing. You can dig much deeper, however, to get all sorts of valuable marketing advice.

On my debrief calls, I started asking questions like the ones below. These inquiries opened up lengthy conversations that led me to previously unknown marketing venues.

- *Do you have any marketing advice for us?*
- *What do you think we should do to get more business from your industry?*
- *What do you think we can be doing to better reach an audience of your peers?*

Step 70. Build Case Studies

As discussed earlier, case studies are powerful sales tools, but there is some legwork involved in creating them. Fortunately, creating case studies is a great excuse to keep up relationships with your customers and secure repeat business. In your debrief, set the expectation that you will follow up for results. Make it easy for your customer to gather metrics and other details by providing step-by-step instructions.

- *I'm proud of what we created, and I hope it serves you well. I would like to create a case study about the project and your company. I think it will be a win-win. Would you help me out with that?*
- *It's very helpful for us to know how well our products serve our customers. With that in mind, I'm wondering how you will be measuring success?*
- *Is it okay if I follow up with you next month to learn what the results have been?*

Step 71. Provide a Take-Home Guide

Many companies don't go far enough to assist their customers after the product is delivered. Once you develop materials that customers can continually reference, they will be more likely to return to you.

Since every product is different, there is no one-size-fits-all approach for creating a take-home guide or other helpful materials. Some products entail long-term consulting and others can be explained with much less. That being said, here are some ideas:

- **ROI Calculator**

   As discussed earlier, this is a step-by-step guide allowing customers to calculate ROI, or otherwise measure the results of their engagement with you. Money doesn't have to be the only metric; you can consider things like positive responses, signups, or improved test results.

- **Inspirational Use Cases**

   Offer examples of how previous customers implemented and measured the impact of your product. Make sure the examples are specific and actionable, and not too sales-y.

- **Resource List**

   Offer a list of sites and articles related to your product and industry. Include brief descriptions of each. Ideally these are resources that will help your customer understand and use your product.

- **Intros to Previous Customers**
  Go a step further and offer to make introductions to previous customers. Assuming the use-cases are relatively similar, your previous customers' experiences will be valuable to those getting started with your offering. This is a way of networking with your customers, which is a great strategy (more on this later).

Step 72. Leverage Customer Interviews

Ranking successfully for your product's keywords is one of the best ways to ensure a steady stream of leads. Quality links directed to your site continue to be one of the biggest factors influencing how you rank in Google and other search engines. While SEO might be outside your purview, as an account manager you're in a great position to encourage inbound links. If a colleague or outsourced company handles your SEO, coordinate with them.

Chances are you have customers with interesting products or services, and interviews with them are a great way to inspire links and web traffic itself. When you're in your debrief, ask if your customer would be open to a quick interview about what they do. This is usually an easy sell because people love talking about themselves. When you post the interview, make sure to send your customer the link. They will probably share your post and link back to you on their company's site or blog. If not, you're still developing fresh content and strengthening the relationship.

- *We've started chronicling our compelling customers through interviews on our blog. Would you be willing do a short interview?*
- *Would you please link back to us once the interview is posted?*

Step 73. Network with Your Customers

Many account managers treat their customers like precious gems, and they store them away from their professional groups. They might worry that their customers will be alienated by introductions to strangers, or that someone will steal the business. This fear is unhealthy because there is much more to be gained than lost when you bring your customers into your circle.

In your debrief and other conversations, try to find out what types of companies and individuals your customer wants to meet, and think about how you can assist. Sending your customer to experts when they are in need is much more helpful than shooting them article links or other information. If your customer starts a relationship with the person you introduced, you will forever be the one who made it happen. When a customer joins your network, you go from an outside vendor to a peer. Since people do business with those they know and trust, this is a great development.

- *What sort of companies or individuals are you looking to meet?*
- *Are there any other services you're looking for at the moment?*
- *What can I do to help out?*

Prospecting (Steps 74-93)

I got in early. I spent the whole morning sending emails, following up on the phone, pulling out my hair, and doing what's generally referred to as prospecting, or lead generation. Before I learned a better way, prospecting meant devoting a lot of time to finding and contacting people in various industries, without rhyme or reason. I wasn't having much fun with this side of the job. I knew it had to be done, but I didn't know how much of "it" was truly needed.

Depending on your product, prospecting might mean cold calls, emails, trade shows, and/or networking mixers. Regardless, it's a numbers game. This fact might make the task seem even more daunting. After you digest the numbers and get an extra hand, however, the impassable mountain will become a scalable hill.

At first glance, this section might seem irrelevant if your duties don't involve lead generation, but stick with it! Even if you're not tasked with prospecting, these steps will give you highly effective research methods, email templates, and tips that you can use in a variety of situations.

Step 74. Set Ideal Goals

When you're facing a long-term task, it helps to cut it down to bite-size pieces. First, make your prospecting goals specific. They should be challenging but attainable. Start from the end goal (closed sales) and trace the funnel to what's required on a daily basis. Here is a step-by-step process for setting goals:

A. Set a Monthly Sales Goal.

B. Determine your Average Deal Size.

C. Determine your Target Close Rate.

D. Determine your Target Conversion Rate. This is the percentage of prospects you expect to move from your Target List into your Pipeline every month.

E. Calculate your Target Monthly Deals by taking A/B.

F. Calculate your Target Pipeline Prospects by taking E/C. This is the number of people you expect to move from your Target List to your Pipeline every month.

G. Calculate your Target Monthly Cold Prospects by taking F/D. Your cold prospects are those you contact who you don't know. They start in your Target List.

H. Calculate your Daily Cold Prospects to contact by taking G/20 (twenty is the typical number of business days in a month).

As an example, let's say Lisa has a Monthly Sales Goals (A) of $100,000 and an Average Deal Size (B) of $25,000 for her intranet development offering. After reviewing her sales history, she sets a Target Close Rate (C) of 10%. She guesses that she will be able to convert 3% of the people in her Target List (D) to her Pipeline. By dividing her Monthly Sales Goal (A) of $100K by her Average Deal Size (B) of $25K, Lisa knows that she will have to win at least 4 deals per month (E). She calculates that she will need 40 prospects (F) in her Pipeline every month by dividing her Target Monthly Deals (E) by her Target Close Rate (C): (4 / 0. 10). Next, she figures out that she will need to contact a total of 1,334 cold prospects (G) every month by dividing her Target Pipeline Prospects (F) by her Target Conversion Rate (D): (40 / 0. 03). Finally, she divides this number by 20 to determine that she will have to contact 67 cold prospects everyday.

When you set your own goals, make sure to plug your numbers into Excel or Google spreadsheets so you can see how changing different factors affects the others. You can get a head start with the Google spreadsheet in **Resources**.

The Daily Cold Prospects target above, albeit hypothetical, might seem like a pretty big number. This is why you should consider outside help. At the end of this section, you will learn how to do lead generation with virtual assistants.

Step 75. Create Prospect Profiles

You have established ambitious but attainable goals for your prospecting efforts, and now you need to figure out who you're going after. Don't fall into the trap of trying to envision every individual or situation served by your offering. Instead, determine the general profiles of your buyers across different industries. These are the "sweet spot" verticals where you're likely to win.

The profile approach is effective because it allows you to hone in on your target's identity so you can envision email outreach templates and other materials. Also, when you're in a networking situation, your profiles will let you better describe your targets to your peers (we'll cover this in the next section).

Use your existing customer base to determine 2-4 profile groups. Some possible criteria for these groups might include business size, industry, title, age, and gender breakdowns. Make sure to note which of your products best fits each profile group.

For example, let's say Lisa sells custom intranet development services (an *intranet is defined as: a local or restricted communications network, especially a private network created using World Wide Web software*). She creates the below profiles.

Each group is tied to a particular product and revenue source. This helps you determine the ROI of your prospecting efforts. Our friend Lisa might observe a slightly higher response rate from Profile A, but she chooses to invest most of her time in Profile B given the higher revenue.

Profile A:
- **Company type:** medium-sized companies; 50-500 employees
- **Industry Sweet Spots:** tech startups, local hospitals, small factories, regional restaurant chains
- **Product:** Standard Intranet Solution - $$ Moderate Price $$
- **Titles:** CEO, COO, President
- **Age:** 30s-50s
- **Gender:** 70% male / 30% female

Profile B:
- **Company type:** Fortune 50; 10k+ employees
- **Industry Sweet Spots:** banking, manufacturing, retail
- **Product:** Premium Intranet Solution - $$$ High Price $$$
- **Titles:** Head of HR, Chief Communications Officer
- **Age:** 40s-50s
- **Gender:** 30% male / 70% female

Step 76. Create Prospect Identities

Next, go a step further and assign fictional identities to your profile groups based on the people who typically inhabit these roles. This exercise will let you develop a closer connection to your prey. Use real customers to inspire these fictional identities.

Profile A:

Lawrence, CEO, age 29

Lawrence is the CEO of a medical technology startup. It's his second venture, and he has recently landed series A funding, which allowed him to grow his team to 50 people. Coming from an engineering background, Lawrence enjoys getting involved with the company's major technical projects.

Marital status: Engaged
Yearly income: $100,000, but he is looking to draw more from the company next year.
Examples of Lawrence in our customer roster: Brian Temporosa of Rendevooz. ly, Joel Whorley of InteliWallet. io

Profile B:

Brianna, HR Manager, age 35

Brianna is a department chief for the HR sector of a Fortune 500 company. Her focus is on employee engagement. She is seldom as-signed technical projects. Brianna doesn't consider herself 'tech-nical,' but she's really glad to be working on something fresh and challenging... it's a bit more exciting than what she usually does. Brianna is affable and hyper-organized. She's mid-career.

Marital status: Married with young children.

Yearly income: $75,000

Examples of Brianna in our customer roster: Mark Stewart of Johnson & Johnson, Marie Khan of Avnet, Elise Richardson of Quiznos

---

Step 77. Write Good Emails

You have probably received this common email from a selfish salesperson:

Hello [Target]:

Our company is [Name]. Your company is doing something wrong when it comes to [marketing, SEO, utilities payments, cake baking...]. We can do it better. Did I mention how much you're messing up? Now allow me to indicate that this is a canned message and that I'm completely ignorant about your company. Here is more information on what we do....

- *Irrelevant thing we do very well.*
- *And another.*
- *And another.*

Call us back. Love us. Buy from us. Please ... buy from us.

"Sincerely,"
Sales flack

Naturally, when I started writing my own cold emails I wanted to get as far away from the above message as possible. Here are the main points to keep in mind when writing an email template:

- **Keep it Short:** respect your recipient's time by stripping out everything that isn't absolutely necessary. Short emails look natural and are more likely to be read.
- **Personalize:** always include the recipient's name, but also make sure to mention their company and other specific references that show you did your homework.
- **Offer Value:** your experience with a competitor or another company in the recipient's arena is often a good fallback. We'll explore other ways to offer value in the following steps.
- **Turn off the Pressure:** don't make the recipient feel like there are strings attached to the simple act of responding to you.
- **Flatter and Be Humble:** imply to the recipient that you're going out on a limb by contacting them. You're not a selfish sales flack shooting emails into the ether. You're putting your pride on the line by initiating a conversation with a stranger because you think their work is compelling.
- **Start a Conversation:** many experts suggest including a call to action requesting a call, meeting, or whatever it is you're going for. I've had more success taking a stepping stone approach: first, get your recipient engaged in an email conversation, then make your ask in the second or third email. It's easier to get a commitment when you ramp up to it instead of making a big ask right away.

Here is an example from Lisa:

Hi Lawrence,

We've been big fans of Health365 since we read about you guys in Inc., so I thought I'd take a chance at reaching out.

We create custom intranet platforms. We've worked with companies like Central PA Healthcare and Doylestown Hospital. Since these organizations are in your arena, I thought it might be worth your time learning about our recent projects with them. Regardless, you can check us out here to see what we're about: www.CompleteIntranetSolutions.com.

Just wondering - have you ever used an intranet platform at Health365? If so, what has your experience been like?

Best,
Lisa

Step 78. Show Your Prospects How to Measure ROI

Now that we've covered the blueprint of an effective cold email, let's focus on ways you can increase your conversions by offering value. Before the digital age, salespeople offered value by providing information about products. Now that information is a commodity, there's a perception that you can learn what you need to know without a biased salesperson.

Offering value nowadays requires creativity. Instead of pamphlets and other "sales collateral," offer your prospects helpful tools. One of the most powerful is an ROI measurement guide, which is re-contextualized from the Take-Home Guide (pg. 79) discussed earlier. Again, the ROI calculation doesn't have to be monetary; it can be based on other things, such as employee engagement or survey feedback.

Step 79. Use Quora for Inspiration

A highly effective method for offering value is clearing up common areas of confusion. Quora (www.quora.com) is a sophisticated question and answer site, and you can use it find topics that bewilder your target audience. You can then write articles and develop helpful materials based on these confusing areas, and you can use them in your prospecting efforts. When you answer questions on Quora, make sure to always be helpful and non-self-promotional. If nothing else, it's a great place to spark ideas and establish yourself as an expert.

Step 80. Send Video Segments

Video is more likely to be clicked and watched than text or static media. Also, video allows a lot of details to be communicated quickly. Try creating a helpful video series on concepts related to your industry. Lisa, for example, might choose to create a 3-episode series entitled "What to Consider Before You Build a Custom Intranet Platform."

Step 81. Interview Your Prospects

As discussed earlier, interviews are a great way to build relation-ships and boost your SEO. It's an enticing way to get people en-gaged with you and your offering. Try using this tactic for prospects as well as customers.

Step 82. Curate Articles

Considering the mountain of information related to complex offer-ings, many potential buyers get intimidated, and they lock up. To prevent this effect, help your prospects by making their research easy. Compile and offer a list of unbiased articles and reviews, and update your list every so often. Once you create this asset you can repurpose it and get a lot of mileage out of it.

Step 83. Keep Timing in Mind

One morning, I was delighted to get a call from a valuable prospect in the health and life sciences industry letting me know that he was ready to move forward with a large engagement. After a long sales cycle, I forgot our first conversations, so I started digging through the history to find out what went right...

First I sent an email that was crafted and tweaked from A/B testing (we'll talk about this later). A month went by, with no response. Then, when perusing my inbox one morning, an alert popped up in the corner of the screen. It was a Yesware notification (more on this in the next step) letting me know that the email had been opened. He was perusing my message, which was a strong sign that something was brewing. I used it as an opportunity to call him and catch up. From there, we entered the running for the project, and soon became the shoo-in. It would be the first of many jobs from this customer.

When doing research, many consider the "who" but neglect the "when." Contacting your prospect at the right time is doubly powerful than simply finding the right person. With that in mind, consider these questions about timing when you're doing lead generation:

- At what stage of life is your customer's company when they need your product?
- What crisis is your customer experiencing when they invest in your product?
- What funding or revenue goal must your customer reach before they can invest in your product?
- Is there seasonality with your customer's buying cycle?
- How long before your customer will be willing and able to re-purchase?

Step 84. Use Timing-Based Tools

Next, consider tools that offer timing-related information about your prospects. Though there are many paid and free resources for all sorts of industries, please see below for a few good ones. You can learn more about these tools in **Resources**.

Yesware

A Gmail app that provides real-time notifications when messages are opened and links are clicked. Also, it lets you store and use templates related to prospecting, Pipeline, objections, and any other category you set up. You can then A/B test different templates to determine which one is most effective.

Crunchbase.com

A startup-focused network of company profiles, Crunchbase tracks funding rounds. You can also find information on executives and board members. When a company is shot up with a $50-million investment, don't you think they'll be in the market for new toys?

Newsle

An app that syncs your contacts and lets you know when people in your life come up as news results. As such, Newsle will alert you to mergers, new product rollouts, press releases, and other major developments with your customers and prospects. When these things happen, extending a simple "congrats" works wonders.

Step 85. A/B Test Your Emails

That which is measured is managed. As you send emails, you will begin to develop valuable data. As described above, Yesware is a good tool for stacking templates against each other.

When you A/B test, make sure to change prominent aspects of your templates, like the subject line. Focus on response rate instead of open rate because it's much more revealing. If you do decide to examine open rate, start by testing a personalized subject line versus a non-personalized subject line, such as "Intranet Services" vs. "Intranet Services for [RECIPIENT'S COMPANY]" (usually the latter wins, but not always).

Build your templates around your <u>prospect profiles</u>. (pg. 85) Lisa, for example, will test competing templates with respect to her medium-sized company targets. Results from other prospect groups won't apply to her findings.

Lastly, gather enough data for each test. I usually determine results based on 50 or more emails.

Step 86. Use LinkedIn to Find Super-Relevant Targets

LinkedIn is one of the most useful networks for lead generation. That being said, its power often goes underexploited.

LinkedIn prospectors make the common mistakes of casting their nets either too wide or not wide enough. 50 super-relevant targets is an ideal goal. This is a number you can work with over the course of a day or two. Taking a small-bite approach lets you narrow your research and quickly determine what's working and what's wasting time. Here's how to find 50 super-relevant targets:

1. Using the Advanced Search function, plug in 5-20 target companies. This number will vary depending on the size of the companies you're going after, but ultimately you'll need to

start with a pool of 500-2,000 prospects. You'll get better re-sults by plugging in specific companies than you will letting LinkedIn search by size, industry, or other parameters.

2. Enter appropriate titles in the "Title" space. Use Boolean phrases to include multiple options (i.e., ["account manager" OR "account director"]). Make sure to select "Current" as employment status.

3. Test out different titles and companies and see what results you're left with. Filter the results until you have 50 super-relevant contacts.

4. If LinkedIn conceals a last name, showing only initials, simply click on a "related contact" in the bar to the right of the pro-file. The full name of the person you're looking for usually pops up as the related contact's "related contact."

5. Find as many email addresses as possible, and discard those you can't track down (we'll get to this next).

6. Log those you find in your Target List.

Step 87. Find Emails with The "Rapportive Trick"

As you know, prospecting is a numbers game, and success comes from connecting with lots of people. Social media platforms offer tons of ways to message your prospects, but email still reigns su-preme. Though Twitter has its uses, everything is public, and serious business conversations eventually leave the platform to continue on other channels. LinkedIn InMails often go unread, and they re-strict your ability to include links and other features.

The typical inbox is a noisy place, but we acknowledge the messages that break through the cacophony. We appreciate those who find us and provide value. This is why cold emails work. In fact, email marketing has 2x higher ROI than cold calling, networking or trade shows (source: MarketingSherpa). Since email can produce great rewards, it's natural that there is a barrier to entry. This barrier is the hunt for addresses.

If you Google "find any email," you will get a bunch of methods for tracking down addresses. The following instructions are not meant to encompass every tactic under the sun, but they are approaches that offer the best results for your time investment. The size and nature of your prospect's company should determine the research method you choose. With respect to small companies, the Rapportive Trick is an effective tactic (source: Distilled. net).

1. Snag a Gmail account and install Rapportive, a Gmail app that pulls in social media data about your contacts.
2. Load the most common email permutations using an email permutator program, which creates different variations based on common conventions (i.e., denglander@acme.com or dan@acme.com).
3. Cut/paste the email permutations into the "To" field of your email. Scroll over the addresses. The Rapportive field will load a name, and usually a pic with social profiles, when you scroll over a correct email address.

In **Resources**, you can find more information on Rapportive, as well as link to an email permutator program

Step 88. Use Search Modifiers for Large Co. Addresses

The Rapportive Trick works when you're targeting a company address that is tied to a social account. Since employees of large companies avoid linking their work email addresses with social profiles, the RapportiveTrick is less effective. The good news is that large companies usually keep the same email convention across the whole organization, so when you uncover one you have cracked them all.

Here is a quick guide to finding email conventions for large companies:

1. Get handy with Google search modifiers. Search for email addresses listed on your target company's website to find the convention they use. Scroll through a couple pages of Google results. An address will usually pop up.
   Try searching for: site: companywebsite.com + email OR contact OR "get in touch"
2. Search for press releases. They often have a contact email address in the footer, which will let you know the convention. Alternatively, you can use PR Newswire (www.PRNews Wire.com).
   Try searching for: site: companywebsite.com + "press release"; company + "press release"
3. Once you nail the convention, test the email address with a verifier program (example: www.verify-email.org)

4. Some email domains will be different than the company's main domain. If your email fails the verify test, consider either the umbrella organization or a subsidiary that your target might be associated with.

5. Once the address passes the test, take a shot at sending a message. Go ahead and send 2-3 more to other targets within the same company. Wait a few minutes to make sure your messages don't bounce back.

Step 89. When in Doubt, Pick Up the Phone

If you're not getting anywhere, move on to a new target and circle back to the problematic prospect later. Since you're dealing with a numbers game, your focus should be on efficiency. If the above methods fail, pick up the phone. Ask a receptionist for your target's email address. If he or she asks why you're contacting them, say, "I wanted to respond to [name] regarding [whatever it is you sell]." Don't spout sales jargon or lies, but give the impression that you're continuing a conversation. Remember, receptionists are there to help, and all you're asking for is an email address.

Step 90. Send One Follow-Up Message

Sending one follow-up to a cold email makes a huge difference. The follow-up lets the recipient know that a human (and not a robot) is on the other end. The follow-up is much more likely to get a response than your initial message. It can be something along the lines of the following:

Hi Prospect,

I thought I'd check back once more on this before I close the file for now. Please let me know your thoughts.

Thanks!
-Account Manager

Step 91. Use Social Media to Show You Exist

LinkedIn and Twitter are great for putting a face to a name, which can have a powerful effect. Follow your prospects and their companies on Twitter before you make first contact, and connect on LinkedIn after you have a conversation.

Step 92. Assess Government Opportunities

Most account managers aren't aware of the lucrative long-term opportunities found in government work, a sector that comprises a major slice of our economy. You don't have to be Boeing or Dyn-Corp to get a piece of the pie. Though the process of landing government jobs is a book in itself, I'll impart some tips for getting to the starting line:

- Get up to speed on the alphabet soup of organizations and processes the government uses to hire vendors. These include CAGE codes, DUNS, SAM, and GSA.

- Sign up for a free trial of a database that collects government jobs. Most of the databases are offered by companies that do business-to-government (B2G) marketing, and "sherpa" you through the process of becoming a government-approved vendor. Learn more in **Resources**.
- Talk to a salesperson at one of these sherpa companies. Though you should be skeptical of custom reports and other upsold products, the people at these companies are a good resource for learning about the B2G process.
- From your database research, determine targets for prospecting. It's tough to land business directly from government when you're new to the arena, so first try reaching out to companies that are landing government jobs. There are often opportunities for partnerships and filling in gaps they do not cover.
- After you have seen potential for government work, consider GSA (General Services Administration) certification. GSA is basically the government's yellow pages for vendors. Because it's a lengthy and relatively expensive vetting process, most companies hire a sherpa company to lead them through it. Once you're in, there are major long-term rewards.

Step 93. Prospect with a Virtual Assistant

Once you crunch the numbers, you may find that you do not have enough hours in your day to effectively prospect. Thankfully, setting up a virtual assistant, or VA, is relatively inexpensive and straightforward.

You can hire VAs on a full- or part-time, or ad hoc basis. If full- or part-time, most VA services require a minimum investment of 20 hours per week, which ranges from $150-$300/week. A hiring service can be valuable because they will handle the hiring process and will streamline free or low-cost trial activities until you find the right person. If a VA is not working out, they will be on hand to find a replacement.

Alternatively, if you're not ready to invest in a full or part-time commitment, you can hire on an ad hoc basis using a service like Odesk or Elance. There you can post a specific activity and pay a nominal rate. Many people find long-term VAs this way, but it may take a few trial activities before you find someone who is up to snuff. Also, if your VA becomes unavailable, you will have to go through the process all over again.

You can find hiring sources, as well as helpful courses on leveraging VAs, in **Resources**.

Though there are VAs based all over the world, India and the Philippines are the major hubs. I've had the best experience with the latter because of higher English language proficiency and similar cultural norms to those of the United States.

Start by looking for VAs with experience in lead generation. Though the skill is often touted, few can do it well. Look for VAs with experience with products that have comparable complexity to yours. Read between the lines to make sure they have experience with independent research, and not just glorified data entry.

For the trial activity, provide your potential VAs with one or two prospect profiles. Describe the profiles in detail via a Skype call, and ask your VA to reiterate over voice and email. As your VA gets started, ask that they send you an update on progress after 2-4 hours.

Get your VA walking before they run. As such, piecemeal the task and make sure they can fully comprehend and execute each part. Start them off on prospect research, and ask them to find 20 super-relevant prospects using the techniques discussed throughout this section. Then ask them to find 40, and then 60. Once you trust them, provide your VA with a company email address and ask them to contact a few prospects each day, with you cc'd or bcc'd. Increase this number as they demonstrate proficiency.

Networking (Steps 94-102)

The phone rang one afternoon. It was the head of a boutique ad agency: "Hi, it's so-and-so. So-and-so sent me your way, and we're interested in learning more about your services." Within a day, they enlisted us to create an event video for a major hotel chain. From an outsider's perspective, this sale probably looked easy. Well, it was and it wasn't; the engagement was the product of months of networking. One intro lead to another, culminating in a successful referral to the agency who called on us when they were in need.

Networking can deliver huge returns, but it involves more than showing up to events, chatting, and exchanging business cards. This section will impart the steps needed to build a strong network that pays major dividends, and it will help you decide if networking is the right strategy for your offering.

If you're not involved in hunting new business, you should still consider networking. A network of trusted peers can help you find ways to serve your customers better and grow as an account manager. A network is invaluable for filling all sorts of personal and professional needs, like finding a new job when it's time to move on. Since building a network takes time, it's never too early to get started.

Step 94. Be Generous

I've attended my fair share of one-sided networking meetings. I sat down for what I hoped would be a meaningful conversation, only to find a sales pitch. My mind fell on one objective: escaping as fast as possible.

When it comes to networking, those who are generous succeed. With that in mind, you should attend your one-on-one meetings with at least two thoughtful introductions for your peer. If you don't understand their business well enough to make good intros, then ask questions like the ones below to learn more.

- *Who are your typical buyers?*
- *Who introduces you to your typical buyers?*
- *What is the sweet spot of your business?*
- *At the moment, what sorts of people or companies are you interested in speaking with?*

Step 95. Be Specific About Your Customers

Nearly as aggravating as a sales pitch ambush was enduring those who were unable to describe their customers with specificity. When I asked the question, "Who are your customers?" I received vague references to general industries. Often I heard, "anyone and everyone." Even if this is technically true, it's an unhelpful answer.

Make it easy for people to help you! Be specific about your customers. This is a straightforward task after you develop your prospect profiles (pg. 85), as discussed earlier. When in doubt, focus on the sweet spot of your business.

Step 96. Be Specific About Your Referrers

For a long stretch, I met with lots of people and followed my above advice. Unfortunately, I received few good referrals. After getting constructive criticism, I realized I was failing to identify and describe my referrers. Referrers are the people who typically introduce you to your customers, but who don't necessarily buy from you themselves. I reviewed my history of closed business, and picked out several referrer groups. I created referrer profiles in the same way I created prospect profiles. They included creative services staffing people and accounts people at web design shops. After identifying and describing my referrers, I started receiving relevant referrals, which led to a lot of new business.

Take a look at your history of closed business. Identify what businesses or individuals could have actually or hypothetically introduced you to each customer. Use this information to create 3-4 referrer profiles. Practice verbally describing them in your networking meetings, and ask your peers for criticism to make sure you are being clear.

Step 97. Avoid Irrelevant Meetings

You can only maintain a limited number of relationships, and there are better uses of time than pursuing every whisper of networking opportunity. When someone offers an intro, be honest about whether or not you think it would be purposeful. If you're not sure, ask the referrer to send you the person's LinkedIn profile or their website link. If you're still on the fence, agree to a phone call instead of a meeting. If you want, claim the usual "busy" excuse. Remember to return the gift of honesty by asking your peers if your intros will be helpful before you make them.

Step 98. Exchange Advice with Your Peers

Although the above lesson is important, you will invariably find yourself in meetings where business opportunities seem doubtful. That's okay! A major ancillary benefit of networking is learning from the experience of other professionals.

Try to get value out of every meeting you find yourself in. See what advice you can gain and what advice you can give. Ask what online tools your peer uses, find out about his or her experience with local groups, or find out if he or she knows a decent paella recipe.

Step 99. Get Constructive Criticism

In the structured groups I attended, and most others out there, the attendees go around a conference table and introduce themselves. Everyone gives a short pitch, describing their product, customers, and who they are looking to meet. Like a high school class, I observed that in any given group there were a few A+ spiels, a few F's, and a lot of B's and C's. Everyone thought they were in the A+ group, including yours truly. The quality presentations were obvious because they got the group's juices flowing and they elicited immediate referrals. Crickets answered the substandard intros, which came from veterans and neophytes alike.

Thankfully, I was able to get constructive criticism about my networking pitch. In response, I rewrote it to focus on why it is we do what we do (revisit the importance of "why" on pg. 45). Next, I got specific about my customers and referrers. Lastly, I kept people engaged by keeping my presentation short. As a result, referrals and closed business significantly improved.

Networking is too time-consuming to be squandered by a bad pitch. Surround yourself with people whose opinions you respect, and then request constructive criticism about your pitch and overall networking approach. It will pay off in big ways.

Step 100. Understand the Types of Groups

There are many venues for perfecting the art of the schmooze. I've been through a gauntlet of groups in the process of building a network that can deliver high-quality referrals. I found that most groups fall into one of several categories, which I've detailed below. These categories will help you better understand the networking ecosystem and pinpoint what will be a good fit for you and your offering.

Individual
These are platforms that line up professionals for one-on-one meetings. They are like dating sites for business people.

Broad
These groups have a general sales focus, and they allow broad admittance. They might include anyone from yoga instructors to bankruptcy lawyers. They are generally very structured.

Professional Offerings
These organizations cut out some of the low-price consumer offerings, and focus on professional products or services. Most businesses in these circles are above a certain price threshold. These organizations tend to emphasize business-to-business offerings, or high-end business-to-consumer.

Same-Buyer-Targeted
These join people who are targeting the same or similar buyers, but don't compete. As an example, a Same Buyer group might target

Fortune 500 CIOs. The group might include a boutique IT implementation firm, a SQL server database management company, and a Cisco hardware distributor. These groups are great for fostering a sense of camaraderie and helpfulness among like-minded hunters.

Buyer Direct

These are groups intended to give the seller face time with the buyer. Since buyers like to avoid sellers until they have an immediate need, these tend to be exclusive and expensive. An example is a large trade show where you find a mixed bag of buyers, sellers, and browsers.

Tangential

These are trade organizations, meetups, thought leadership groups, and other organizations that influence or at least interest your customers. Your customer will attend these groups from time to time. For example, if you're selling a social media monitoring platform to large advertising agencies, a tangential group is the Advertising Research Foundation (ARF). The ARF collects and shares insights on consumer research, and its attendees include strategists from large brands and agencies.

Step 101. Assess the Pros and Cons

As for the pros of networking, the prospects that are sent your way will be much easier to close because of the trust element that comes from personal introductions. Also, networking caters to recurring revenue in certain business ecosystems. For example, real estate brokers, lawyers, title insurance brokers, and others in real estate continually drive each other's businesses because each party plays a part in a large transaction. Networking offers the ancillary benefit of keeping your social muscles strong. It lets you keep your finger on the pulse of your profession. When you need advice, recommendations, and other outside help, a trusted network is extremely valuable.

As for the cons, networking requires you to attend frequent events, meet one on one, and follow up with introductions. You have to continue this process over a long period to develop meaningful relationships. These factors make networking time-consuming. It's difficult to scale because it's almost impossible to replace yourself in a face-to-face environment. Finally, there tends to be an urban focus to networking, and it's difficult to sustain if you're not based in a major city. Though there are remote networking options, they tend to be less powerful.

Step 102. Figure Out if Networking Is Right for You

Networking proponents will tell you it's the single greatest sales driver you can adopt. This is true in some situations and untrue in others. Networking's success hinges on the nature of your offering, your schedule, and your personal affinities.

If you put in the time, generosity, helpfulness, and you can describe your offering effectively, then your networking efforts should eventually deliver business. You should expect nothing less.

That being said, getting relevant referrals for complex, non-transactional products can be challenging. If you're a commercial real estate broker, your network refers those who want to rent space for their companies. There is a well-defined and universally understood need for your service, and it's transactional. If you're an account manager for a custom intranet solution catered to the Fortune 500, you're in a different boat. Your product is based on the project experience. It's complex and non-transactional.

To figure out which boat you're in, answer True or False:

A) Most people understand what your product does.
B) You have to give a detailed explanation before people understand your offering. Often this requires multiple conversations.

A) After you first describe your product, everyone knows who your customers are.
B) An in-depth description is needed before people understand who your customers are.

A) You can throw a rock and hit your customer.
B) Your customers have specific titles in a few specific verticals.

A) You sell a product or service.
B) You sell the experience of a project and the deliverable that comes from it.

If you answered "True" to 3 or more of the "A" statements, you probably sell a transactional product. It's something people generally understand. You will get big returns from networking if you put in the time and effort.

If you answered "True" to 3 or more group "B" statements, you're likely selling a complex, non-transactional product. You will need to educate your network about your offering before you can expect relevant referrals. Though building a network may produce dividends, it will be a long-term process. If you do decide to give networking a try, make sure to diversify your efforts with other sales channels.

Conclusion

Who would want to be an account manager, anyway? Excellent question! The role offers many opportunities for personal and professional growth. Account management touches on the most compelling aspects of sales, project management, client services, marketing, and other areas. Whether you're a newbie or a veteran, there's always something new to learn.

Being a great account manager means making everyone happy all the time, which probably sounds impossible. Thankfully, you can get close to this divine state, and you can do it while working reasonable hours. Being successful means being systematized, which isn't so hard once you drill down to specific steps.

I hope my book finds you more business, happier customers, and less stress. Regardless, I know it will give you the insight I wish I had from day one.

Key Takeaways

- Batch your tasks and limit email; stick with your mission, not with your schedule.
- Understand customer expectations so you can manage them.
- Be your customer's advocate before, during, and after the engagement; adopt a villain if needed.
- Put out fires by offering options; keep a foibles list; be clear and firm about your process.
- Systematize sales using 3 lists: Pipeline, Target List, and Farming List.
- Systematize customer service using checklists like those made in Asana.
- Continuously qualify your prospects and make sure you understand their buying situation.
- When you give your pitch, focus on the "why."
- Close prospects by defining what "closing" means.
- Respond to objections by admitting that you might not be the right fit; use the low-pressure atmosphere to explore every opportunity to make something work.
- Ask for referrals before and after a customer engagement; conduct a debrief call to explore future opportunities.
- Set ambitious but attainable prospecting goals, and drill down to specific numbers; get help from a virtual assistant.
- Be a generous networker; get constructive criticism to refine the way you describe your customers and referrers; consider the nature of your product and personal affinities to decide if networking is your best time investment.

Additional Resources

If you want to boost your sales and delight your customers, then please sign up for our newsletter. It will keep you up to speed on new tools, apps, and strategies. Also, I'm very excited to announce that I will be offering video courses and one-on-one consulting. These options are perfect if you are looking for a hands-on approach to sales and account management. In the newsletter, you will find discounts and updates about these forthcoming opportunities.

Go to www.SalesSchema.com and click "Join Our Newsletter"

Thanks so much for reading, and I look forward to hearing from you!

-Dan Englander
@DansPalace

Acknowledgements

Experience is a big concept, and without getting into the semantic weeds, it's mostly determined by the people in your life. You can divide that group in two: those who help you, and those who don't. I'm blessed to be surrounded by the former...

- Will Gadea, for your leadership and steadfast vision for a successful company, one that's as much determined by its culture as its business strategy. From your tutelage, I will one day write the Great American Email. And a hat tip for the prospect profile approach.
- Mike Gansl, for being a real *macher* and always saying the things that needed saying. This book would not have happened without your guidance and inspiration.
- Mike Fishbein, for all the ideas, resources, and feedback related to all things marketing and self-publishing.
- Brett Donjon, for being a meticulous copy editor and bringing this thing home.
- Louis DeNicola, for being the library that is you, and letting me pick your analytical mind for the last few years. Thanks for always coming to the apartment with beer in hand.
- Brian Erickson, for giving me my first foray into the wild world of New York networking; I'm glad I wasn't the only freakishly tall person in the room.
- Sean O'Rourke, for always "poking the bear," and a hat tip for articulating the "Adopt a Villain" concept.

- Robert Kopecky: Thanks, amigo, for reminding me not to sweat the small stuff. Also, gracias for the only meaningful "two groups of people" line.
- Gideon Kendall, Dana Wulfekotte, Jacques Khouri, Brad Matarazzo, and all the talented artists at IdeaRocket for making my life easy by allowing me to sell and manage a quality product.
- SaraJane Askildsen, for your organized mind, and for helping me learn by teaching.
- Brian Temporosa and Eric Blevens, for being strata-geniuses and fast tweet deleters.
- Luke Stets, for showing me a world of possibilities by always being up to something interesting.
- Eric Wilson, for being a great sounding board. I look forward to more crazy ideas from the both of us.
- Andrew Lawton, for your in-depth and very constructive suggestions.
- A huge thanks to all other customers, partners, friends, and acquaintances who provided valuable feedback throughout the course of this project.
- Lastly, thanks to Casey for distracting me in all the right ways at all the right times.

About the Author

Dan Englander is the founder of Sales Schema, a site that helps professionals achieve their goals by finding the right balance between sales and customer or client service. Previously, Dan was the first employee at IdeaRocket, an animation studio specializing in commercials, explainer videos, corporate industrials, and other video projects. As Senior Account Manager, he won new business and managed accounts for a large and diverse client roster. Dan started his career at DXagency, a boutique digital marketing firm. He lives in New York.

Made in the USA
Lexington, KY
07 August 2018